GREAT WHITE
STURGEON ANGLING

Bud Conner

Frank Amato
PORTLAND

Published in 1996 by Frank Amato Publications, Inc.
P.O. Box 82112, Portland, Oregon 97282
(503) 653-8108
amatobooks.com
ISBN: 1-57188-067-4
UPC: 0-81127-00110-1
Cover and back cover photos by Steve Conner
Photos by the author unless otherwise noted
Map and book design: Charlie Clifford
Printed in Singapore
3 5 7 9 10 8 6 4 2

Contents

Dedication:

To the sport of sturgeon fishing and all fishers young and old who practice good sportsmanship.

Bud Conner is a weekend fisherman, the father of five adult children, the grandfather of twelve, and great grandfather of one. Bud makes time to go fishing with one or more of the kids most every weekend.

An undersized sturgeon captured by Jennifer Lawson and Ken Mitchell. It was photographed and released in a matter of moments with the help of a tailer. Larger fish should not be "tailed" like this because it can harm soft internal organs. Handle sturgeon gently and practice catch and release. The more fish we release, the more big fish there will be left to enjoy. Frank Amato

1
The White Sturgeon and its Relatives

The sturgeon family includes the largest fresh water fish known. They are a large ganoid fish, with armor-like scales consisting of bony plates covered with dentine and enamel, living in both the Atlantic and Pacific oceans as well as the Caspian Sea. They migrate into fresh water in early spring through late summer to feed and spawn.

Four sensory barbels are located on the bottom of their snout to aid in locating and identifying food which is rutted out of mud and sand bottoms with their snout. Their mouth is formed so as to be extended, or protruded.

A large female white sturgeon will release eggs sometimes numbering in the millions. Females begin spawning at 15 years of age and need powerful, fast-flowing water (8 to 12 miles per hour) over a rubble (bouldery) bottom. Depending on various factors, females do not necessarily spawn each year. They broadcast several hundred thousand to several million eggs which hatch about a week after fertilization. Two months later the fry will have reached a length of five and a half inches.

After about a year, they go to the estuary and sometimes roam up and down the coast frequenting bays and estuaries.

A Few Different Sturgeon Species

Throughout the world there are about 30 different species of sturgeon. The Columbia contains two species, the white and the much smaller and rarer green which stays in or near saltwater.

Acipenser oxyrynchus, the common sturgeon of the Atlantic coast, ranges from the Gulf of St. Lawrence to the Carolinas, and

After you have caught a couple, you will quickly fall in love with the mysterious sturgeon. Frank Amato plants a kiss.

FRANK AMATO

Marty Sherman displays a Tillamook Bay sturgeon before release

occasionally is found in the Gulf of Mexico. It is also present in European waters.

Acipenser sturio, another sturgeon of the Atlantic Ocean, was once common in the Hudson River, but over-fishing and water pollution have nearly destroyed the fishery. Their red flesh was once so common on the market, it was often referred to as "Albany beef". It is also found in Europe.

Huso Huso (also called the beluga) is the famous sturgeon of the Volga River in Russia, which is the major source of European caviar. (Columbia River white sturgeon was equal in quality when it was available from large fish in the past.) Large specimens weighing over a ton have been slaughtered for their eggs, nearly destroying that fishery. The record *Huso Huso* was 28 feet long and weighed 2,800 pounds.

Scaphirhynchus, the shovel nosed sturgeon, is a much smaller species, seldom exceeding five feet in length, and is found in the Mississippi River system.

Acipenser fulvescens is found in the Mississippi and in the Great Lakes. The hackleback or switchtail also can be found in these inland bodies of water.

Acipenser brevirostris is the short nosed sturgeon and ranges from Cape Cod to Florida. It is very small (up to two feet long) and not much is known about it.

Acipenser transmontanus, the white sturgeon of the Pacific Ocean, is the largest of the species in the Western world, and is honored with titles such as, "Sacramento", "Pacific White", "Oregon" and "Columbia River". This famous and prolific sturgeon ranges from the Sacramento River north to Alaska and reaches lengths of over 15 feet.

Acipenser medirostris, the green sturgeon of the Pacific Ocean, is easily distinguished from the Pacific white by its olive green appearance and its longer snout and inhabits the same range as the Pacific white although it stays in brackish water where it spawns. It is not prolific and is seldom caught. Maximum size is about four to six feet.

It is truly amazing that a fish hatched from an egg the size of a mustard seed can grow to 15 feet or better in length, weigh a ton or more, and live to the ripe old age of 200-plus years. *Acipenser transmontanus*, the white sturgeon of the Pacific Ocean, and *Acipenser Huso*, the famous sturgeon of Russia's Volga River, are the two largest sturgeons of the species that fit that description.

A word of caution to the sturgeon angler. For protection sturgeon have five rows of bony scutes. These spurs are sometimes razor sharp and can leave the unsuspecting angler with a handful of tiny, painful cuts. A sturgeon's barbs and spurs are not poisonous, but will leave cuts susceptible to infection from river water. Consider using gloves and a net or tailer when handling sturgeon. The smaller the sturgeon, the sharper the spurs. Grasp smaller sturgeon around the head, covering the eyes to calm it, while removing the hook.

Although sturgeon enter coastal rivers to spawn in early spring and return to sea in late summer, a large population remain as residents in some of the larger rivers, providing a year-round fishery.

Russia's Caspian Sea is the world's largest inland body of water. It is nearly the size of the state of Montana, and is 770 miles long and 300 miles wide at its northern end and reaches 3,072 feet in depth in its southern part.

The sea is 85 feet below the level of the greater oceans and has an annual rainfall of 8 to 10 inches. It is almost totally dependent on contributing river systems. None of the water of this system ever reaches the greater oceans; it is totally self contained.

Food fishes include Caspian roach, shad, blackback, and Volga and Dolgin herring (sounds like a pretty good diet for sturgeon).

At one time this river and sea system contained five different species of sturgeon, one of which is now extinct. Over-fishing of *Acipenser Huso* for its world famous caviar and pollution threaten it with extinction.

In addition to over-fishing, water pollution and over-fishing of bait fish can easily upset the food chain and do great harm to the sturgeon population. Although sturgeon have a reputation for being ancient survivors, upsetting the delicate balance of nature can force them into extinction.

Columbia River white sturgeon, often referred to as a living fossil, are a carry over from prehistory and have rapidly become one of the most popular sport fish in the Pacific Northwest as fewer salmon return to their spawning grounds each year.

My first encounter with "the mighty toothless one" took place back in the fall of 1953 in a small northeastern Oregon town by the name of Halfway which sits in a scenic valley about 60 miles northeast of Baker City, near the deepest canyon in North America—Hells Canyon.

Great uncle Bill Brokaw, a veteran of World War I, lived down Hells

Great uncle William B. Brokaw who introduced me to the wonderful world of sturgeon fishing in the fall of 1953.

PHOTOGRAPHER UNKNOWN

Canyon several miles downriver from Robinette, Oregon in a tumble-down shack a stone's throw from the Snake River. Bill would show up in Halfway nearly every Friday, and that evening when he negotiated the hairpin curves of Pine Valley Grade in his coughing, wheezing old Model A Ford, I would be with him, looking forward to a weekend of doing chores (chopping wood, milking the goat, checking the trot lines and maybe helping strain the latest batch of elderberry wine). I later came to the conclusion that in reality that old veteran only wanted some company.

One November day to my delight Bill showed up on Thursday. This time he was driving an old Buick chopped down to a pickup truck and in the bed lay the most awesome creature I had ever seen. Bill explained that it was a sturgeon, and it didn't hurt a thing that the tail of that big fish had been dragging the highway all the way from his house to Halfway! I figured that helping Bill butcher it was far more important than going to high school, so the next morning we hauled it out in the valley and next to Pine Creek together we butchered it. That evening I had my first taste of sturgeon, a steak as large as a dinner plate.

Growth Rate

The growth rate of white sturgeon varies considerably depending on water temperature. In warmer water they can grow at the rate of one foot per year for the first three years. In the cooler waters of the Columbia they grow at a much slower rate. It takes a Columbia River white sturgeon nine years to reach the length of three feet, 13 years to reach four feet, 21 years to reach five and one half feet and 24 years to reach six feet.

Sturgeon are normally opportunistic bottom feeders. But they are not limited to bottom feeding. They eat mainly ghost and mud shrimp,

This juvenile sturgeon washed up on a boat dock during a stormy August night in the Columbia River Gorge. had it survived and gone on to become one of those 15 foot ocean-going spawning giants, it would still have the same number of bony plates and spurs as in its infant stage. The large spur-tipped plates (scutes) running from head to dorsal fin number from nine to 13. The other four rows of plates and spurs remain the same in number too, they only grow larger, smoother and spread out as the sturgeon grows older and larger.

crawfish, sculpins, herring, smelt, shad, salmon, lampreys and clams. No wonder I enjoy eating the sweet and firm white meat of Pacific sturgeon.

Sturgeon also target and pursue live prey. On several occasions I have had sturgeon chase my bait up to my boat as I reeled it in. Once I caught a large sturgeon when my bait was a good 20 feet off the bottom and moving.

I like to cast downstream from my boat, allow my lead to hit bottom, then "walk" it back an additional 100 feet or so. I have boated a lot of good-sized fish using this method. Sturgeon will often take the bait as it is drifting along the bottom.

It is my firm belief that the methods and techniques explained in this book can be applied to sturgeon fishing in any water sturgeon populate, whether angling for Pacific whites or any of the four species of sturgeon that inhabit Russia's Volga River. About the only variation would be the bait used which should be native to the water being fished. For example, Columbia River smelt works quite well in that rivers system, whereas imported smelt from the Great Lakes seems to be pretty much ignored. Lamprey should work equally as well in Atlantic Coast waters as it does in Pacific Coast waters because lamprey are native to both bodies of water. The same can be said for shad.

Winte stur- geon spawn in very few rivers along the Pacific Coast. Spawning sturgeon are very particular in their needs which include a very large flow of water moving from eight to 12 miles per hour over large, bouldery rubble. The spawn is broadcast into the flow and the small eggs sink to the bottom and hatch in about a week. The only rivers known to host spawning white sturgeon are: the Fraser in British Columbia, the lower Columbia below Bonneville Dam and also The Dalles Dam and the Sacramento-San Jaquin system near San Francisco Bay. Sturgeon migrate from these areas into tidal water and bays and into the ocean but generally not very far and they always return to them for spawning purposes. Because some fish wander in their search for food, bays such as Tillamook, Grays and Coos (to name only several), contain whites. These fish are generally of a fairly large size because it appears that smaller sturgeon do not wander long distances.

Popular Rivers and Bays

2

FRASER RIVER: The Fraser is a very large, fast and powerful river that drains much of interior British Columbia and is free of dams. It is approximately 630 miles long and enters the Pacific Ocean 12 miles south of Vancouver, British Columbia. Its chief tributary is the Thompson River which is about 350 miles long and flows by the town of Kamloops.

The Fraser River contains many great white sturgeon which feast on the carcasses of millions of sockeye salmon as well as smelt runs and other fish. White sturgeon are spread throughout almost the entire length of the river, however, the major sport fishery takes place in the lower 100 miles of the river from the town of Hope downstream to the estuary.

The largest recorded white sturgeon was captured in this river and weighed over 1600 pounds and measured about 18 feet. In the late 1890s the white sturgeon population of huge, mature fish was decimated in only a few years by commercial fishermen using nets. Since that time the river has been managed conservatively and the sturgeon population has improved. However, in the past several years many huge, old fish have been found dead along the river's shore and fisheries biologists have not been able to determine if these fish died from natural causes or pollution. Currently the river is open to sturgeon fishing on a catch and release, barbless hook basis. For information about sturgeon fishing in the Fraser River contact:

Fred's Fishing Adventures, (604) 858-7344, British Columbia.

COLUMBIA RIVER: The Columbia is 1,214 miles long. The total length of the river in Canada is 459 miles. White sturgeon were historically present in over half of the Columbia's length as well as its major tributary, the Snake River. Today, because of

A great fishing hole located in the historic Columbia River Gorge as viewed from the Vista House which is located at Crown Point on historic Highway 30 (the scenic Columbia River Gorge Drive). Sections of Highway 30 have been preserved and are maintained for access to farms, communities and tourism. Highway 30 provides a doorway to much outstanding scenery, state parks, hiking trails, falls and picnic spots not available on I-84 and is well worth the diversion. (It is a narrow, twisty road and not recommended for larger boat trailers!) If you make this little side trip take a camera.

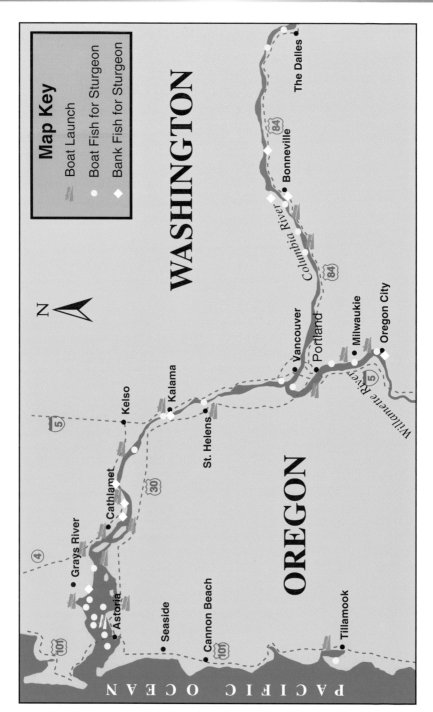

Map Key

- Boat Launch
- Boat Fish for Sturgeon
- Bank Fish for Sturgeon

N

WASHINGTON

OREGON

PACIFIC OCEAN

Columbia River

Willamette River

The Dalles
Bonneville
Vancouver
Portland
Milwaukie
Oregon City
Kalama
Kelso
St. Helens
Cathlamet
Grays River
Astoria
Seaside
Cannon Beach
Tillamook

84
5
30
4
101

A typical summer day in the Columbia River Gorge begins at dawn with little or no wind, builds to a fair east wind, and by midday has shifted to a fair west wind which usually produces choppy water, and by early evening has returned to no wind and a mirror-flat river. These conditions are fairly normal but not always predictable; they don't discourage many sturgeon anglers.

dams, sturgeon populations in much of the upper Columbia above The Dalles Dam are severely depressed because of lack of spawning areas. Below Bonneville Dam the sturgeon population of fish over two feet long is estimated by sturgeon researchers to be about one million fish. If Bonneville Dam had been built just five miles downstream of its present location it would have destroyed the sturgeons' major spawning grounds and there would only be a remnant population of big fish left!

The Columbia discharges into the ocean a volume of water ranging from 85,000 to 1,160,000 cubic feet per second (extreme flood conditions). It discharges annually into the Pacific Ocean an average of nearly 160,000,000 acre feet of water. It is the largest river on the Pacific Coast and second in water volume in North America to the Mississippi. Because most of the Columbia runs through high, mountainous country creating a quick fall, the Columbia is the most powerful river in North America—remember this when you anchor up!

SACRAMENTO RIVER: The Sacramento is the largest California river. Its origin is near Mt. Shasta in the northern part of the state. A short distance south of Sacramento it is joined by the American River,

A typical winter morning on the Willamette River, a mirrored "flat" river, broken only by an occasional passing barge or a lone fishing boat. The Willamette presents an extreme danger to anchored fishing boats from barge traffic and an added danger from tankers and large transport ships. A series of five blasts from a larger vessel's air horn means danger; at this signal it is wise to pull anchor and move on—no matter how many blasts you may hear!

its main tributary, and then continues southward, entering Suisun Bay, unites with the San Jouquin River, follows a strait into San Pablo Bay and then empties into the Pacific Ocean at Golden Gate.

Other popular Pacific Coast sturgeon fishing bays and rivers are: WASHINGTON: Willapa Bay, Grays Harbor and the lower Chehalis River, the Snake River (catch and release only). OREGON: Tillamook Bay, Yaquina Bay, Coos Bay and Rogue River estuary. CALIFORNIA: Klamath River. IDAHO: Snake River (catch and release only).

Not all rivers, estuaries and bays that white sturgeon inhabit are named here. Any river with appreciable depth from San Francisco Bay to the Skeena River in British Columbia will contain sturgeon at one time of the year or another. Sturgeon are opportunistic feeders and range around looking for food. Don't be afraid to try new waters or something different in the line of bait.

WILLAMETTE RIVER: The Willamette River originates south of Eugene, Oregon and flows northward through the lush Willamette Valley where it joins the mighty Columbia River north of Portland at

Kelley Point. The Willamette is 190 miles in length and is the second largest tributary of the Columbia River in terms of yearly discharge. Draining an area of only 11,000 square miles, nevertheless it has the national distinction of carrying the most water for a river completely contained within the boundaries of one state with flows sometimes exceeding 150,000 cubic feet per second!

Willamette Falls is a natural barrier to sturgeon, however, the Oregon Department of fish and Wildlife has released thousands of small sturgeon upstream to create a new fishery.

Because of high and steep Willamette River Falls at Oregon City, sturgeon historically were only in the lower 20 miles of river. Sturgeon have been released above the falls and perhaps in time a good fishery will develop as presently occurs in the lower 20 miles. The Willamette River has a fresh water tidal estuary of about 20 miles (to the base of Willamette Falls), effected by a small tide at Portland, and provides a year-round fishery for sturgeon and an enormous annual spring run of spawning shad and lamprey eels which is probably the main reason for the sturgeon population below the falls. It is also believed by some anglers that big sturgeon spawn in the forceful flow below the falls, for many small fish are in evidence as well as the occasional "monster" fish.

3

Tackle and Rigging for Bankers and Boaters

Bank Fishing

Bank fishing for sturgeon is entirely different than fishing from a boat. The rod and reel are considerably different as are the rigging and technique.

The ideal bank casting rod is 14 feet long and one piece with ceramic or aluminum oxide guides combined with a good heavy-duty, wide-spooled bait casting reel. There are many reels on the market to choose from. For bankers I recommend the Daiwa 58, Shimano 20 40 and the Penn 25 GLS, all deliberately without a level wind in order to reduce line friction so that you can make a long distance cast. With a bait casting reel some of us end up with a "birds nest" that would attract a bald eagle. I include myself in that group of bank casters. For those in that group I recommend a good heavy-duty spin casting reel.

For several years I made good use of an old Daiwa spin casting reel which held about 250 yards of 40 pound test mono line. That old reel was my favorite for both boat and bank. I used it until the bail wore through. It was a sad day when that old reel finally gave up the ghost and found its way into the trash barrel. I don't even remember the number of that old Daiwa, but I do know that when it comes to rods and reels, Daiwa is a good name to keep in mind.

Now I have a Daiwa Sealine 250H with a graphite frame, a solid wide spool and no level wind with a 3.5 to 1 return; a Daiwa Sealine 30H 3.5 to 1 return, no level wind; a Penn Peer 309 with capacity for 350 yards of 40 pound test Maxima Tournament Silver mono line; and a Penn 49 deep sea reel which has a deep, narrow solid spool, mounted on a 5 foot roller-guided glass rod designed for fast water boat fishing with steel line.

The purpose of a sacrificial weight is to insure that it will snag on the bottom where you want your bait to stay put, instead of having it wash downstream only to end up next to shore.

Once the weight is firmly anchored to the bottom of the river, the line is reeled in tight enough to "cock" the rod. A sturgeon will pick the bait up and run with it, the dropper line will break and the fight is on. The cocked rod will snap back when the dropper breaks, the sturgeon setting the hook with its weight against the snagged sinker.

Many bankers attach a small bell to the tip of the cocked rod and go about their business of talking, reading, napping or whatever, and

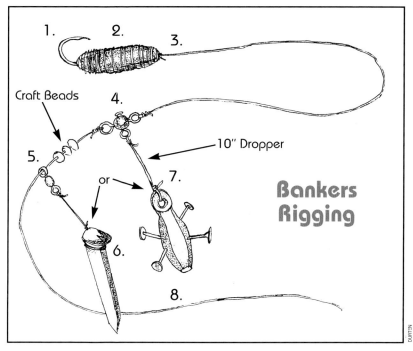

1.
2.
3.
Craft Beads
4.
10" Dropper
5.
7.
or
Bankers Rigging
6.
8.

DURTEN

1. Lamprey chunk or bait of choice wrapped tightly to hook.
2. Use elastic thread to secure bait tightly to the hook. 6/0 to 9/0 size barbless hook is recommended.
3. Heavy nylon or leader of choice.
4. Three way swivel with break-away dropper to weight.
5. Sliding 2/0 swivel with short break-away dropper to weight.
6. Railroad spike or lead of choice. Use No. 6 or No. 7, never both.
7. Bank casting lead with 16 penny nails embedded to ensure a snag.
8. Good quality 40 lb. test mono line.

wait for the wake up call. Believe me, a bank fisherman will come alive at the sudden jingle of a bell!

I can't be held responsible for what might take place should some practical joker decide to pull such a foul deed on a tired bank fisherman catching a few well deserved winks at home on the couch.

Many of us are not able financially to charge out and spend three or four hundred dollars on a custom made 14 foot sturgeon rod and a top of the line reel. Fortunately there is an alternative. You can purchase for under a hundred dollars a decent salmon rod and reel combo, a spool of good quality mono line, a spool of No. 18 Mason's braided nylon line for leader, some 2/0 swivels and some cannon ball sinkers and some 6/0 to 9/0 barbless hooks.

A rod and reel designed for salmon fishing is actually a good outfit for both bank and boat sturgeon fishing alike, the only difference is

The butt of the rod during a battle with a good sized sturgeon. Notice that the butt of the rod is firmly planted in the bend of my hip. Using this method can result in a serious groin injury. Consider using a fishing belt. The belts shown are homemade from a couple of old automobile seat belts, PVC pipe and epoxy putty. They are quick and easy to put on and quite comfortable to wear.

the terminal rigging and technique.

The bankers' rigging illustrated in this chapter is for the purpose of fishing in fast water. A more ideal rigging for fishing in calmer water is a bank casting lead minus the nails, or a cannon ball lead on a slider as in the boaters' rigging illustration.

Boat Fishing

Boat fishing for sturgeon differs from bank fishing mainly in the type of rod used. The ideal boat rod is about seven feet long with a fairly sensitive tip, with a lot of backbone through the handle, fiberglass construction with ceramic guides, combined with a good heavy duty reel with the capacity to hold at least 250 yards of 40 lb. test mono line. The reel should have a smooth working, heavy-duty drag. Make sure the fiberglass rod butt extends through the entire length of the handle. I once experienced the disappointment of losing a rod and reel when an oversized sturgeon made an unexpected change of direction and I was left holding the handle of one of my favorite sturgeon rods.

Improved Clinch Knot

Hook Snell

1 **2**

3 **4**

1. Pass 10 inches to a foot of line into the top of the hook eye, lay the line along the shank and form a loop approximately the same length as the hook. Grasp the eye of the hook and wrap the loop over itself around the entire hook. **2.** After making 6 to 8 wraps around the hook shank, grasp the line near the bend of the hook at the point where the last wrap was finished. Your wraps will extend from the hook eye down toward the bend. **3.** While still holding the last loop firmly against the hook to prevent unraveling, slowly pull the line above the hook until the remaining loop tightens against the wraps. **4.** Trim tag against shank.

Palomar Knot

Blood Knot

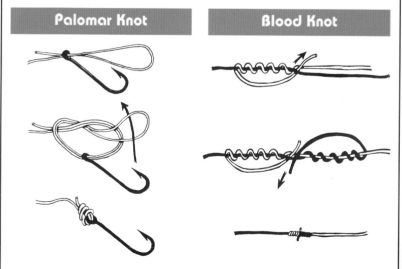

BILL HERZOG

Boaters—Rigging for Sturgeon
A Sharp Hook Makes the Difference

Make a needle of stiff wire for threading leader through shad, lamprey "eel" and smelt. Elastic sewing thread and large craft beads can be purchased from any fabrics store.

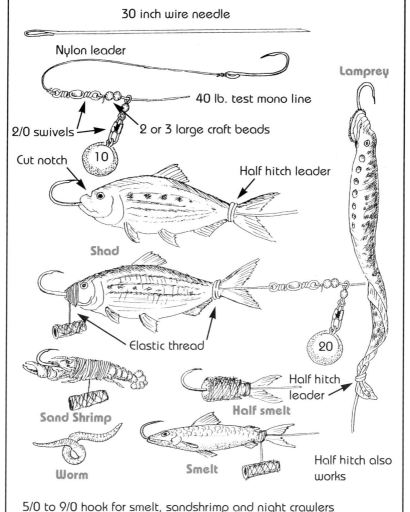

30 inch wire needle

Nylon leader

Lamprey

40 lb. test mono line

2/0 swivels

2 or 3 large craft beads

Cut notch

10

Half hitch leader

Shad

Elastic thread

20

Sand Shrimp

Half hitch leader

Half smelt

Worm

Smelt

Half hitch also works

5/0 to 9/0 hook for smelt, sandshrimp and night crawlers

Earl Conner nails a 7-1/2-foot beauty using shad for bait.

This is a good example of an exposed 11/0 hook on about 3 feet of one eighth inch braided nylon line threaded through a full shad with a 20 oz. cannon ball lead attached to a sliding swivel slider on 40 lb. test Maxima line.

For boaters rigging for sturgeon a sharp hook makes the difference. Make a needle of steel wire for threading leader through shad and lamprey eel. Elastic sewing thread and large craft beads can be purchased from any fabric store.

Good quality boat rods available on the market for under a hundred dollars include the seven foot Daiwa Sealine, the seven foot Shakespeare Ugly Stick Tiger and the Penn Power Stick. Any of these rods will make a good sturgeon rig when coupled with a good reel such as a Daiwa Sealine SG40, Penn 320 or a Penn 330 ranging from about $80 up.

The boat fisher doesn't rely on a bell to let him know he has a fish on, he is usually found with at least one eye glued to the end of his fishing rod waiting for the slightest indication of a sturgeon mouthing the bait.

Do not hide the hook, sturgeon are not hook shy, nor are they leader shy. Keep in mind that if you carefully conceal the hook inside your bait, when you detect a bite and set the hook, more often than not, your bait will simply pull out of the sturgeon's mouth. No matter how soft the bait my be, your hook will have to penetrate the bait before it can hook the fish, and that split second will often make the difference between just a bite or a fish on.

Hide the hook and you will often find yourself saying "I should have had that one, I felt him." Or, "That was a good bite, I don't know how I missed it?" (You pulled the bait out of the sturgeon's mouth just in the nick of time!) Keep your hook sharp and keep it exposed, that's the difference between a good bite and a fish on.

Use a good, tough leader. I have been very successful using No. 18 braided Masons nylon line. I prefer nylon leader because it tends to stretch under stress. A rigid line is more apt to break under stress and mono will not only break, it will cut into a sturgeon, should it roll up in your line, as they often do.

Sonar

The constantly changing and advancing technology in the field of sonar and electronics has provided the boater with valuable aids in reading the ever changing bottom of rivers and bays and in locating sturgeon.

My old 18 foot Olympic is equipped with an Eagle Z-5000, an older model, and I sometimes find it difficult to distinguish between river debris and fish, although this is of little concern because I seldom use it to locate sturgeon, I use it mainly to read the bottom. For example I look for places where sturgeon are most likely to be feeding. My depth finder will bounce back a signal showing about a 30 foot circumference, depending on the depth, and I will be fishing well out of that range. I find it quite productive to locate a deep hole or channel and drop anchor above, below, or to the side, bait up and give it an honest chance (this can take a lot of patience, but sometimes proves to be very productive).

Fishing deeper holes, as in a back eddy, can also be productive, although you will more than likely spend a great deal of your time releasing small shakers. I refer to these places as nursery holes because I believe that juvenile sturgeon spend most of their time in the relative safety of deep, dark holes where they find an abundant supply of food. Don't get me wrong, larger fish hang out in the same areas and you can catch some nice fish as well as shakers. You can also hook into a lot of snags and lose more than your share of hooks, line and sinkers. Food for sturgeon is not the only thing that drops into these holes.

Of course one of the secrets to experiencing a successful fishing trip is to fish where the hungry ones are, and a good depth finder with the capability to locate and identify large fish hugging the bottom can prove to be a valuable aid, although I have yet to see a depth finder that can distinguish between a hungry sturgeon and one that has a belly full. Sturgeon are not always hugging the bottom. One good trick is to locate sturgeon, determine the depth they are holding, motor upstream until the bottom reads the same depth, drop anchor well enough above that area so you will be fishing at the same level, and then wait for the critters to find your bait.

*T*here are literally dozens of baits that white sturgeon will happily eat. However in the Columbia River and its estuary there are several favorite baits that stand out.

Sturgeon Baits

4

Lamprey

The Pacific lamprey is a primitive eel-like fish which feeds by attaching itself to a host and sucking its body fluids. In spring the adult lamprey enters rivers to spawn in large circular nests usually near tailouts and often in salmon or steelhead redds, which it makes by removing stones with its mouth. Lampreys die after spawning. Native peoples and others consider lamprey a delicious food fish. Sturgeon dine on lamprey at every opportunity during the spawning season, it is an excellent bait to use at that time of year. Slice it and place it on your hook. Use a whole lamprey if you are fishing for big whites. Often you can buy it frozen.

This huge sturgeon wanted a whole shad bait.

Smelt

Columbia River smelt, or eluachon, (*Thaleichthys pacificus*), is a delicious food fish that ascends many Pacific Coast streams to spawn. The Columbia River in late winter and spring hosts runs numbering in the tens of millions. Sturgeon love fresh or frozen smelt. This is an excellent bait to use anytime of year and is generally always available at bait shops.

Shad

Several million shad enter the Columbia River in spring (May, June, July) and migrate and spawn up to 400 miles upstream after ascending several dams. The young drift to sea in late summer and live there until mature. Shad feed on plankton and when mature are from 15 to 24 inches long. They are a food fish and both flesh and roe are eaten. Atlantic shad were introduced into Pacific waters in 1871. Anglers armed with light tackle tipped with shad darts line the rocky shoreline below Bonneville Dam and at numerous other hot spots downriver.

The Willamette River is also famous for its shad run with anglers lining the banks and hog lines of boating anglers anchored at Clackamette Park during the annual shad run.

The extremely large shad runs in the Columbia are one very important reason the river has such a large population of sturgeon.

Whole shad are used by anglers searching for giant sturgeon. Smaller pieces of shad can be used for regular-size sturgeon. Whole shad can be bought in some tackle shops or you can catch your own and then freeze them.

Shad have helped foster the growth of sturgeon back to a healthy population. But if shad ever become a popular and marketable fish, then sport anglers will have to band together to stop commercial fishing or heavily regulate it.

It is best to carry a variety of bait in your bait bucket or cooler, of course the bait should be kept on ice during warmer weather. That old bait bucket can get to be a real stinker in hot weather; it seems there is always someone aboard who can't remember to close the lid!

There is such a large variety of stur-

The cover photo shows a 14 foot sturgeon caught on a sand shrimp no larger than a man's finger. This photo shows a juvenile sturgeon caught on a shad nearly the same size as the sturgeon. This confuses the old saying "big bait for big fish—small bait for small fish."

When you drop that big chunk of bait over the side all sorts of critter want it. Sculpin like to peck away at the soft belly of a smelt. upon the approach of a sturgeon, however, the smaller pests desert the bait.

geon bait available it is difficult to carry all of it on any one fishing trip. Use the bait of the day or whatever seems to be producing best. Most sturgeon fishermen will tell you what is working; you need only ask. When smelt are spawning, use smelt. When shad are spawning, use shad. When lamprey are spawning, use lamprey, etc.

During the shad run, many sturgeon fishermen spend the first hour or so shad fishing for bait then head for their favorite sturgeon hole and spend the rest of the day sturgeon fishing.

Shrimp and Other Baits

Other good baits include: anchovy, herring, herring roe, squid, sand shrimp (ghost shrimp), mud shrimp, crawfish, nightcrawlers, sardine and many different varieties of pickled fishes such as herring, sardine and shad. These and other baits can sometimes be scented with all types of concoctions available in bait shops, such as anise which is probably the most popular

Years ago I pickled some shad filets in a very strange brine. Not having the proper spices or vinegar for my recipe, I decided to improvise. While searching my pantry for vinegar to use as a brine, I came upon several jars of home-canned jalapeno peppers that my daughter Pamela had put up for me.

Those peppers were so hot they could melt dentures; I had placed them in a safe location deep on the top shelf in a "keep out of reach of children" (or any human being!) location. Anyway, I decided to use the vinegar from those extremely hot peppers as brine for my shad filets. My filet of shad is a very thin, tightly rolled strip consisting more of skin then flesh and makes a good pickled bait. I allowed that concoction to marinate for nearly a year (refrigerated) before trying it as bait for sturgeon. To my surprise, sturgeon seemed to love it, I couldn't keep 'em off the hook! So like I say, don't be afraid to try something new.

A red and swollen vent on a sturgeon does not always mean that they are feeding on fresh water clams—it can sometimes mean that they are feeding on crayfish, such as the claws and other parts of the

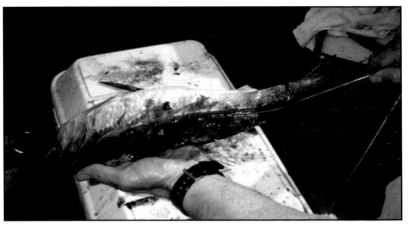

Whole shad are used by those who are targeting big sturgeon from six feet on up in size. Here the back of the shad is being removed with a knife in order for it to bleed and thus attract a giant whites interest.

shell. Crawfish are a major part of their diet in the Willamette especially from November through February. The crawfish population is concentrated mainly in shallower water from 10 to 40 feet deep and with a rocky bottom.

Feeding sturgeon are more difficult to locate in the Willamette then in the Columbia and you will need to move quite frequently at times in order to find a concentration.

I have found as many as 15 crawfish in the stomach of a Willamette sturgeon ranging in size from one to several inches. Sturgeon pursue and eat live crawfish as well.

I have never caught a keeper or outsized sturgeon on a crawfish, although I have caught many small sturgeon on the white meat taken at the tail of the crawfish. Maybe if I were to pursue the use of such bait a bit more I might be successful with large fish. I have caught all my keeper-sized Willamette River fish on the following baits: Columbia River smelt, sand shrimp, shad strips, pickled shad, pickled herring and night crawlers.

A Salmon Smolt Surprise

Not wanting to upset those who insist that sturgeon are not a threat to salmon smolts, I have evidence to the contrary going back some 25 years ago while fishing the shallow waters of the Columbia River from the shoreline of Rooster Rock State Park. My brother-in-law Matt and I would head up river every chance we got, armed with our salmon rods, spin casting reels and a can or two of nightcrawlers.

We would hang a worm or two on a 5/0 or 6/0 hook, tie on a 10 inch "dropper" tipped with an 8 ounce bank casting lead, and cast as far as we could, prop our rods on what ever was handy, and wait for the bite.

The fishing was always good and the catching was sometimes good, although most of the catch was small shakers. Sometimes we would get lucky and head for home with a "keeper". My point is that every fish we took was full of fingerling salmon!

More of the same evidence has come to my attention in the last couple of years while on fishing trips further up the Columbia in the Dodson area, out from The Fishery. While anchored in a productive hole the bite would be on and we would observe an Army Corps of Engineers barge dumping its load of juvenile salmon and within minutes the bite would be off. Every time this would happen, we would move around from one good area to another, until we would find a spot where the bite was on again. We would usually head for home with at least one keeper and discover fingerling salmon in its stomach, every time!

Sure, Army Corp fish barges each year save millions of salmon smolts from being chopped to bits from the spinning turbines of Bonneville Dam, but then they are released smack dab in the middle of a major feeding grounds for gulls, squawfish, smallmouth bass and sturgeon.

Salmon smolt is no bait! It is illegal to use fingerling salmon for bait and is unnecessary with all the legal baits available.

The Bite

Usually when a sturgeon is mouthing your bait the "bite" is very subtle. Often it will be similar to a crawfish, chub, or squawfish after your bait, but it is most likely to be a sturgeon.

That subtle nibble is what I call an indicator. When you detect the indicator immediately tip your pole down with the tip next to the water, giving your line two or three feet of slack, and wait until you can feel the sturgeon pick up your bait. You don't want the sturgeon to feel any resistance while it is taking the bait. They will usually spit the bait if they feel any resistance.

If you feel the sturgeon picking up the bait, set the hook. By setting the hook I mean to yank your pole to a full upright position as though you were trying to break it, then crank down until the tip of your pole is near the water and wait to feel movement on the other end of your line. If you feel the fish on, set the hook one more time and begin the pump and crank method, allowing no slack in your line until you take your fish off the hook.

You never know whether you have another undersized "shaker" or an oversized prehistoric monster fish on until you set the hook. A ten-foot sturgeon will nibble at the bait so gently that you will think it is just another baby sturgeon.

5
Where to Find Fish and Guides

I like to drop anchor in a prospective area, tie on a bait that I figure the fish might be feeding on, cast a short distance downstream, walk it back a little farther and wait 15 or 20 minutes; after trying a different bait if I still am fishing a dead hole I'll pull anchor and move to another prospective spot—sometimes 50 or 100 feet away, sometimes several miles up or downstream.

The first fish caught is seldom big. If small shakers are being caught it's worth the wait for a bigger one. Where there are little ones there are smaller ones, sometimes bigger ones and occasionally oversize fish.

One clue as to where to fish is to check your catch. Look at the vent. If it is red and swollen then most likely it has been feeding on freshwater clams. If most of the shakers you catch appear to have been feeding on clams it is wise to move to the clam beds which are usually in shallower water (30 or 40 feet deep) with a sand bottom. Sturgeon plow the sand bottom in search of clams and will gorge themselves. They digest the meat inside and pass the empty shells causing red and swollen vents.

Another way to determine where to fish is to observe other boaters. Experienced fishermen return to areas that have been productive and you will generally find boats grouped in those areas. I choose not to use that method. If you do, be aware of a couple of things: consider where the other boaters' anchors and anchor lines are, how much anchor rope may be out and where their fishing lines are. In anchoring near other boaters take into consideration the depth of the water, the current and its swing and the force and direction of the wind. Placing an anchor requires much thought and good judgment.

I prefer to keep a healthy distance between my boat and other boats for another good reason: If a sudden squall should develop and you are anchored in a group of boats you just might find yourself in serious trouble. I recommend, especially in the Columbia River Gorge, that you try at all times to keep a safe distance between your boat and other boats—both when anchored or moving.

There are certain areas which fishermen refer to as "most productive", but in reality these places are everywhere. You can catch sturgeon in 10, 12, or 90 feet of water.

A while back I took my brother Donald with me on one of my

Looking up the east ramp at The Fishery; hidden among the trees is the campground area. The background cliffs demonstrate how the Columbia cut its way through the Cascade Mountains on its way to the Pacific.

The Fishery (formerly Coverts Landing) sits on the south bank of the Columbia, some 30 miles east of Portland, in the world famous Columbia River Gorge. There is a bait shack with fishing tackle, gasoline, ice, snacks, a paved launching ramp, docking and moorage. There is a modest fee for launching.

The Fishery is a great place to spend a summer vacation, campsites are available and include electricity, water and restrooms with hot showers.

fishing trips to the Columbia River Gorge below Bonneville Dam. Don loves boating and fishing but he has a problem with choppy water, just a little rock and roll and all the color will leave his face and he will begin looking back at the dock. He has a serious problem with motion sickness.

Early one morning we motored out of Portland with my boat in tow and headed east on I-84, turned off the freeway about three miles past Multnomah Falls on exit 35, and ended up at the boat landing at The Fishery, and wouldn't you know there was a little west wind.

The Columbia flows in a westerly direction through the Gorge and it doesn't take much west wind to put a little chop on the water. Don looked a little nervous as we launched, but he was still standing there holding the boat when I got back from parking the truck. I fired up the motor and we headed out into the Columbia in search of "old tooth-less".

Don with his two fish limit. This photo was taken when you could still keep two fish under four feet in length. "Can you guarantee this every trip?" said Don, with a sheepish grin on his face!

I tried to find the calmest area and we ended up in a spot in one of the back eddies about 20 feet from shore and in 20 feet of water. I didn't expect to catch anything and sure enough I didn't, but Don did. In the first hour he caught two legal fish! I caught a few shakers. After searching the river for about three hours and only hooking small fish, we headed back to our original fishing hole and immediately I hooked into a really hefty four footer! They are where you find them.

Islands, channels, main current, clam beds, shad, other times of year (winter, spring, summer, fall) Willamette River, Columbia River (from Gorge downstream to Astoria) Charter boats.

Secrets

I have no secrets when it comes to catching sturgeon, I am more than willing to swap stories with anyone. My best advice is that you can catch a lot more fish on a wet line than on a dry line, whether from a boat or from the bank, get your line wet, get out there and do your time. If you are a boater, fish shallow, fish deep, give the sturgeon a chance to pick up the scent of your bait and if your location is not productive move around—they do, and they are always feeding.

The major concentration of oversized sturgeon in the Columbia River (fish from 6 to over 10 feet long) extends from Rooster Rock upstream to Bonneville Dam. Although they are very powerful swimmers and can leap completely free of the water, they seldom travel through fish ladders. Why should they when Bonneville Dam provides them with such a plentiful feeding ground offering turbine chopped salmon and steelhead smolts, millions of shad, lamprey eel and all sorts of other fish.

Here is an interesting tip for baiting smelt. Carefully place the hook through the smelt's head, wrap it tightly to the hook and leader with elastic thread and prepare to make your cast, but wait a second. . .before you make the cast lay the smelt on a rock, cutting board or the boat deck and give it the old 60 pound press—step on it, no—stomp on it!

Make smelt mush of it. I call it a smelt Frisbee. If there are sturgeon anywhere in the area they will find your bait, You will catch a lot more small shakers, but where there are little ones there are often big ones.

A sturgeon has four nostrils and a very keen sense of smell and will follow a scent trail to its source; you can imagine the sent trail a smashed smelt makes with bits and pieces flitting off and washing downstream.

Another effective method is to tear the smelt in half and attach the tail half to the hook with the open end pointed away from you. Another method that works quite well is to bait with smelt and add two or three big, juicy night crawlers on the hook. The smelt should always be rigged with the head pointed away from you; the hook should be exposed enough to add night crawlers. The same can be said for herring, anchovy or other baitfish.

Should You Book a Guide?

If you have not fished for sturgeon before one way to learn quickly about many of the techniques, from fishing to boat and anchor handling, is to hire a guide. Yes, it will cost a few bucks, but the information gained will be invaluable.

Many guides will accommodate up to four anglers to a boat for up to an eight hour day. You can expect to pay about $60 to $150 per person. Some guides will charge less for catch and release.

There are good guides and there are even a few bad guides. You can find sturgeon guides by reading the sturgeon fishing guide listings in *Salmon Trout Steelheader* magazine or other outdoor publications or by calling your local tackle shop. If you are unsure of the guide, ask for references you can call. Most guides are very competent fellows who enjoy teaching and helping you hook fish and understand the lifestyle of the sturgeon.

You should seek a full-service guide—one who provides all the tackle and bait. Make certain ahead of time who is going to bring the lunch and beverages, and don't forget the raincoat.

6

A River Accident & Selecting a Sturgeon Fishing Boat

*T*he newspaper headline read, "Deputy Saves Child In Overturned Boat." It was an unforgettable day in July of 1981, a day everything went wrong.

I launched my old 16-foot wood boat at the public boat ramp at Camas, Washington, with my fishing partner and wife Ann and our four year old grandson Christopher. We headed into the Columbia and set course for Tower Island, a low outcropping of rock on which sets several high power line towers near Sundial Beach.

Ann's sister Trudy and her husband Glenn Polsen were following in their 14 foot fiberglass boat. We decided to drop anchor just upstream from the island and try our luck at sturgeon fishing. Both boats were short on anchor rope, but we decided to drop anchor anyway. We really never gave it much thought, assuming that if we had enough rope to reach bottom it should be enough to anchor up. We had fished that area before without trouble, but on that day there seemed to be a much stronger current than we had encountered on previous fishing trips. After dropping anchor and feeling it drag a short distance and snag up on the rocky bottom, I began having second thoughts about fishing the hole when suddenly my anchor buoy went out of sight under water and didn't resurface.

I yelled to Glenn that the current was too swift and that we should pull anchor and try our luck in another location. After a short discussion we decided that because we were already anchored we might as well fish for a while. After about a half hour of sitting there and trying to keep our lead on the bottom we noticed that my anchor buoy had still not resurfaced, I insisted that we pull anchor. We both began pulling anchor at the same time and that's when all hell broke loose! I fired up my old Scott 60 and began to swing the bow around to get a good upstream pull on the anchor, but with my rope too short and nearly straight down, I couldn't make much of a swing, and suddenly the tired old outboard motor coughed and died, the rope hung up on a stern cleat, pulling the stern under water and it seemed as though the whole damned river began rushing in!

I yelled at Ann to cut the rope but the knife that had been laying there on the deck in plain sight was by now lost in a half submerged boat. After a frantic search she found the knife and managed to cut the rope, throw a life jacket on Chris, and begin helping me bail water (fortunately there were two five gallon plastic pails aboard).

We had no way of knowing that Glenn and Trudy were having their troubles too. They had somehow managed to get their anchor rope wound up in their prop, resulting in yanking their outboard motor loose from their boat before breaking the rope! Then they drifted around the north side of the island and could see the bow of our boat sticking up at a funny angle as we drifted around the south side.

Trudy flagged down a Multnomah County Sheriff Patrol boat, which luckily happened to be cruising by, and reported to deputies Erin Kelley and Tim DeBauw that we were in trouble on the other side of the island.

Deputy DeBauw brought the patrol boat around the island and pulled alongside our boat with intentions of pumping the remaining water from my boat. Suddenly and without warning the stern of my boat went under and flipped the boat completely over backwards! I was thrown clear and the bow came down on top of Ann and Christopher! Ann felt Chris slip out of his life jacket as she sank deeper into the river.

I had been swept several yards downriver by then and found it impossible to swim against the strong current back to my boat. By now another couple had seen we were in trouble and had motored over to help and I climbed aboard their boat.

I turned and looked back at my overturned boat, hoping to see Ann and Chris, but they were nowhere in sight! Then I saw Ann resurface next to my boat and I yelled, "Grab the boat and hang on." By that time Deputy DeBauw had jumped from his boat and swum to her side asking ,"Where's the boy?"

Ann answered, "I can feel him touching my leg." DeBauw swam under water in search of Chris. He was under for what seemed an eternity before resurfacing empty handed!

He again asked, "Where's the boy?"

Ann answered again, "I can feel him on my leg!" DeBauw dove under again using Ann's leg as a guide and found the boy's leg poking outside, grabbed it and pulled, but the boy wouldn't budge! "Using all the strength I had," DeBauw yanked on the leg one more time and Chris slipped through the window. He then carried Chris to the surface, swam to his boat and handed Chris to Deputy Kelley and then swam back to my boat and tied a line to its bow so it could be towed to shore. He then swam back to his boat where Erin Kelley pulled the exhausted DeBauw aboard.

Deputy Kelly had thrown a life ring to Ann during the rescue and she was pulled to safety.

"It was touch and go," DeBauw recalled. "If I didn't get the boy out of there in 30 seconds or so it would have been over." Deputy Tim DeBauw was the hero of the day and will always be our hero!

Christopher, 10 years after his underwater rescue.

Upon examining my boat after the accident I discovered several deep gouges on its bottom near the stern and some damage to the lower end of the outboard motor. This indicated the boat had hung up on an underwater object (probably a rock), causing the stern to be pulled under water.

I share this story in hope that just maybe it will prevent someone else from having to go through a similar experience. This accident was 100% preventable! It had nothing to do with bad luck, it had everything to do with poor judgment and dumb mistakes—mistakes like going boating without the proper equipment aboard—such as a safe anchoring system. Your anchor system should include a break away anchor and anchor buoy and a rope which is at least four times as long as the depth of water in which you plan on dropping anchor.

You should also have a large bailing device (even if your boat is equipped with a bilge pump), proper fitting life jackets and a sharp knife kept in a permanent, convenient location near the stern of your boat so that you can cut the anchor line in a moment's notice.

Tugs and barges, ships, log rafts—these can all spell danger. Be alert and aware at all times. Respect the laws of our waterways and use common sense.

If you are not familiar with navigation and water safety laws, familiarize yourself. Free booklets are available at most sporting goods stores and marinas and through your state marine board.

You might be anchored well clear of shipping lanes and out of the channel and still be in danger of being plowed under by a barge. Be alert at all times. Why argue with an oncoming barge that resembles a horizontal 10 story building moving at 10 miles per hour or more? Its an argument you will always lose.

Beware of the unique danger of tug-pulled log rafts. You may think you are anchored a very safe distance from a passing log raft in tow, and the tug might pass at a safe distance and the main raft might also appear to be passing at a safe distance, but if the tail end of the raft should get caught in a cross current it can swing over and collide with your boat or hook on to your anchor rope. For that reason you should have a quick release anchor set-up so that you can get out of the way fast! But even better—plan ahead!

The only thing that is predictable about the Columbia River, especially in the Gorge, is its unpredictability. Strong currents can and do change direction and the wind frequently changes velocity and reverses its direction, sometimes without warning.

I remember one summer Saturday when we were sitting anchored in the Columbia River Gorge in a light east wind. Suddenly the wind stopped. I kept a watch for an indication of a west wind (because that is what usually happens) but there wasn't a sign of a west wind. We sat there for about an hour in a dead calm. I kept waiting and watching for an indication of choppy water or white capping down river, but no, we remained in a dead calm. Then suddenly a 50 mile per hour west wind sat down on the entire section of the river.

There were over 100 boats out there that day, many anchored in groups. Every boat was immediately in trouble, especially those anchored in groups with their boats banging together and crossing anchor ropes. Everyone was trying to get back to the boat dock at the same time. What a mess. Luckily no boats were lost. I can't stress enough: keep a safe distance from other boats and shipping lanes and stay alert and sober. Alcohol and boating is a very dangerous combination, as are drugs and boating. Many boating accidents happen almost as quickly as car accidents.

The Columbia River has a fast drop to it. In the lower 150 miles from Bonneville Dam to its mouth near Astoria the current can vary from a mild incoming tide to over 12 miles per hour. (Spawning sturgeon like the first five miles below Bonneville Dam because they need water flowing from eight to 10 miles per hour in which to spawn!) Water columns almost 100 feet deep can be moving as quickly as four miles per hour.

Selecting a Sturgeon Fishing Boat

What should you look for in a good sturgeon fishing boat? You need a boat which is comfortable, easy to clean and has ample space to move about when fighting a large sturgeon. Your boat should also offer protection from foul weather with either a small cabin, hard top or cloth top placing you and your partners out of the cold winter wind and rain and next to a propane heater.

You need a boat that will get you out to the fishing and back to the dock or boat launch in a hurry should the weather turn vicious. It should handle well in rough water and not drench your passengers with spray while under way. It should also be stable while resting at anchor or cruising in either calm or rough conditions.

Your boat should give you the feeling of riding in it, not on it. It should be large and comfortable for two or three passengers and the

The Columbia River Gorge near Bonneville Dam.

captain, but not too large to trailer so that you have to keep it moored.

There always seems to be a large market of used boats as well as new boats. Just remember that if someone is selling their boat there is probably a good reason. If it has to do with poor performance you need to know what to look for. Thus it is necessary to take the boat out and put your prospective investment through a series of tests, preferably in windy, choppy conditions. If you do not feel comfortable with your own judgment then take an experienced boating friend along. An ideal test involves a maximum acceptable load aboard because you will probably be fishing with at least one to three other anglers aboard for companionship.

Steering Wheel

If your perspective boat has a steering wheel, controls and captain's seat, there should be plenty of leg room under the wheel and dashboard to allow you to operate the controls without getting your arm in a bind, having your legs go to sleep or banging you knuckles. The captain's seat should not be so close to the steering wheel that you cannot operate the boat from a standing position.

Windshield and Visibility

The windshield should be mounted solidly with a sturdy center brace and two support braces for a split windshield. The windshield should be large enough to see through when you are seated without having your vision blocked by the upper framework. Keep in mind that you may be able to see well while anchored, only to find that your vision may be blocked by the framework when the boat is underway due to the attitude of the boat while in motion. The windshield should have side windows for even more support and to provide protection from wind and spray. Of course windshield swipers are always nice to have, whether manual or electric.

Boat Capacity

The boat capacity plate is usually located near the steering wheel on the dashboard and contains the serial number of the craft along with the load capacity under normal conditions. The load capacity is not determined by the number of boat seats. The load capacity plate isn't there just to look official, or to cover a hole in the dash—it is required by federal regulation and demands your close attention. It is there for your protection. Do not exceed the maximum boat capacity. In fact its safest to stay several hundred pounds short of the suggested maximum capacity. When loading your boat include the combined weight of yourself, passengers, fuel tank, storage battery, motor, gear and anything else of substance.

Boat Tops

A top on a fishing boat provides protection from the relentless rays of the sun as well as from the rain, wind and cold. How nice it is to cozy up to a heater within the protection of a covered boat while keeping an eye out for the subtle tug of a sturgeon bite. A hardtop (generally fiberglass construction) will provide this protective sanctuary and will make for an attractive boat but will restrict your field of battle with a large sturgeon to the stern area while the sturgeon has no limits and might possibly circle your boat and foul the anchor line. A cloth or rag top can be quickly folded out of the way providing you with an unlimited area in which to do battle—assuming you have the time and foresight to unhook your boat from the anchor line.

Static Stability

Static stability occurs when the boat is at rest in the water at anchor. A boat with poor static stability will rock whenever someone decides to get up and move around to stretch or get into the tackle box for new rigging making it very annoying to a fishing partner who is watching for a bite. Static stability will also be tested when a passenger decides to sit on or lean over the gunwale and in extreme cases might give you the feeling that the boat is in danger of tipping over.

Dynamic Stability

Dynamic stability occurs on a good boat when it is under power. The bow will lift and plane across the water, not through it. As the boat gains speed the water under the bow provides dynamic stability. Dynamic stability is broken if the bow remains at an uncomfortable upward angle or if the boat lists to one side. Then the load must be shifted. Both the design of the boat and power of the motor must be in balance to provide dynamic stability.

With the boat under power this is the time to make another simple but crucial test by cautiously removing your hands from the steering wheel to see if it stays on course or severely veers off to the left or the right, potentially placing you in a dangerous situation.

A boat steers at the stern much like an automobile traveling in reverse. It takes little imagination to understand the problems experienced should you drive an automobile 20 to 40 mph or better in reverse! Of course an automobile doesn't have a planing hull, nor does it have the rush of water under its bow to hold it tightly to the road. This leads to another critical boat test—run it through a series of tight turns in a figure eight pattern. Be sure that you have ample room on open water to perform this test! Begin slowly and then continue to slowly increase the speed. If the boat banks into the turn and stays on course, it has dynamic stability. If the stern has a tendency to slide out in the turns, it has poor dynamic stability. A boat that spins out or slides out in a tight turn could slam into another boat or solid object resulting in a serious accident.

Don't make the mistake of assuming that just because a boat is wide across the beam that it has good dynamic stability. The center of the gravity plays a large roll in the stability of a boat. A high center of gravity is very unstable. The lower the center of gravity is, the more stable the boat becomes. If you add a cabin or top to your boat keep this in mind. Consider all the factors before buying or modifying a boat.

Motor Power

Don't make the mistake of outfitting your boat with too much power. The maximum power capacity for a specific hull is contained in the information located on the boat's capacity plate. Overpowering the boat can result in its sinking. It can happen quickly from a standing stop as you accelerate full-out. The bow will not only raise to plane but will continue to climb until the hull is in a vertical position. Then it will react in the same manner as an airplane when it goes into a stall after reaching maximum vertical climb—it will fall back. If this occurs with your boat it will go under at the stern and sink like a rock.

Choice of Boat

My preferred choice is a deep-vee hull boat with good static and dynamic stability, a split windshield providing access to an open bow and cloth top. The hull should be aluminum or fiberglass and I prefer an outboard motor with long shaft and prop for fuel efficiency. I'm

Sturgeon are very sensitive creatures and carefully check-out potential food with sensory barbels. They can become very moody at times and refuse what anglers are sure they'll take!

not happy with anything less than a full floatation compartment under my feet. My present boat comes close to that description. It is on older Olympic deep-vee 18 foot fiberglass hull with a cloth top powered with a 70 horsepower long shaft Evenrude motor. It has the inconvenience of a solid windshield and hatchless bow which is of little or no consequence to me after having learned to drop and retrieve anchor in the manner described in chapter 7.

A standard flat bottom rocker-style drift boat is great for drifting rivers and rapids but makes for a rough, slow ride on choppy water. However, a modified drift-type boat with a wider stern and semi-vee hull with mid-ship controls and retractable cloth top can make an excellent sturgeon boat.

Inboards

The one disadvantage with inboards is that they restrict the open area in the stern because of the motor placement. These boats are very comfortable, however, usually coming with tops and walk-through windshields. Depending on the type, they are very popular for everything from shallow river running to water skiing—and with the proper anchor knowledge you can hook sturgeon from them as well.

Caution: Deer Crossing

This is information every boater should know. Deer know no boundaries and the mighty Columbia is certainly not restricting for the large population of deer that inhabit the forests and islands of the Columbia River. Migrating herds, or even a lone deer, swim across the Columbia. They are adept swimmers and the river poses no threat to them but they are vulnerable when they make this long journey. The threat comes mostly from curious boaters trying to get a good photo or attempting to help an animal that appears to be floundering. This can cause the animal to panic and drown.

When cruising the river keep a sharp eye out for floating debris and keep in mind that the bobbing head of a lone deer may not be very visible in the early morning and late evening hours. If you should be so fortunate to witness such an event, steer clear of the animal and warn other boaters.

Deer populations inhabit both sides of the Columbia from its mouth into Canada in both forested and dry land areas and cross at many places throughout the river's length. Two crossings that I am aware of are by Horsetail Falls and downriver at Dalton Point in the Columbia Gorge.

*T*he anchor
system I use now
was invented by fishermen
for safe deep and/or fast-
water anchoring. It has several
very important features: first, the
boater is able to leave the anchor in
place (when he finds the need to leave
quickly) by simply throwing the entire
anchor line overboard or unclipping from it.
This capability is absolutely necessary for the
purpose of chasing after oversized sturgeon.

Secondly, this system is extremely helpful because
it takes most of the backbreaking work out of pulling
anchor—and in the Columbia sometimes you might have
several hundred feet of anchor line out attached to an anchor
weighing 40 pounds or more! Anyone who has pulled anchor by
hand (especially in cold, fast, deep, powerful water) will fully appreciate this anchor system.

Here is how it works: A large, strong anchor buoy is coupled with
a rope-locking brass metal device which allows the rope to slide
through freely in one direction and lock or grab in the other direction. When lifting the anchor the captain simply motors upstream

*A typical Columbia River anchor system featuring a rocking-chair anchor, about six feet of
chain, an anchor buoy with a metal rope grab, about 350 feet of half inch nylon rope
and a tailing buoy.*

Anchoring in powerful, deep, fast-moving currents takes the right equipment, proper organization and confident execution.

above the anchor's position and the anchor line is pulled through the floating buoy's ring thus lifting the anchor from the bottom and pulling it up to the buoy where the brass metal device locks it. The buoy, obviously, must be large enough to float the anchor. At this point the bow person pulls the anchor, chain and buoy onboard after he has carefully placed the long nylon anchor line in a big plastic bucket.

Nylon rope is best because it is soft and supple, having no memory (it will not return to a former coil in cold weather), has good resistance to the ultraviolet rays of the sun and will not rot. Polypropylene rope costs less money than nylon and will float, but those are the only advantages it has over nylon; it is a bad choice.

The length of chain is necessary to insure that the anchor will tip over and dig in, rather than scoot along the bottom like a couple of skis or sled runners. The chain is connected to the stem of the anchor with a string or plastic cable tie that will break under a heavy pull in the event that the anchor has done its job too well and is stuck on the bottom. When that happens the boat's captain may have to pull in several different directions until the break-away snaps. When the break-away snaps, the force of the pull is transferred from the stem to the bottom of the anchor and most of the time the anchor will break free. No matter how good the anchor may be, or how well it works, there comes a time when it will be wedged so tightly in the rocks, a mass of roots, or other snag, that you have to cut the anchor rope.

The two most dangerous circumstances that get boat fishermen in trouble are anchoring and lifting the anchor! If you find yourself in trouble with the anchor and it is pulling your boat under or severely down, cut the rope, DON'T HESITATE, cut the rope! Always keep a sharp knife in a convenient, permanent location near the stern

Dropping Anchor from an Open-Bow Boat

Dropping anchor in many parts of the Columbia is a two person job. As the bow person slips the anchor over it is his duty to see that the anchor line follows smoothly. It is best to keep the long anchor line (up to 300 feet of line!) in a large plastic bucket so that when it goes out it does not tangle in your feet or on other items near the boat's bow. If the anchorage is in fast water the anchor line must not

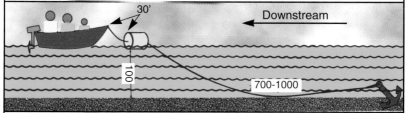

Anchor Safely (Army Corps of Engineers)
Swift currents, high flows and cold water make the following recommendations imperative

Downstream

30'
100
700-1000

1. Use 7-10 times the depth of the water for the length of the anchor line. River depth may exceed 100 feet in some places. Use a float for the anchor line (see the diagram) to serve as a buffer and reduce the risk of getting the anchor line tangled in the propeller.

Lower, do not throw, the anchor and avoid tangles in the line.

Anchor only off the point of the bow. Anchoring off the stern or the side will capsize your boat.

2. Power upstream of anchor before retrieving it. Maintain position in the line with flow of current while retrieving anchor. Turning cross-wise to the current increases the risk of capsizing.

3. The Columbia River can become turbulent with little or no warning. You are advised to wear a Coast-Guard-approved floatation device at all times. Also, take precautions against hypothermia. River temperatures can range from the 70s in the summer to the 30s during the winter.

be allowed by the strong current to drift under the boat and tangle in the propeller. This can be immediate disaster because if the anchor hangs up on a short line the boat will gyrate wildly and then sink like a stone! Before using this type of equipment for the first time practice several anchor drops and lifts in calm water until you have absolute confidence in what you are doing.

Dropping Anchor from a Closed-Bow Boat

Dropping anchor from a closed-bow boat requires a much different method. The stern person drops anchor as the captain operates the boat slowly in reverse.

When pulling the anchor line in fast, powerful water, much care must be given to keeping the anchor line away from the propeller. If you tangle your propeller with the anchor line, immediately turn the engine off and attempt to cut the rope; the faster the water and the shorter the line to the anchor the more dangerous is your situation; that is why you should not attempt to anchor in fast water until you have absolute confidence in yourself and your anchor mate. If the anchor is stuck in fast water then it is best to go far upstream for leverage when using the boat's motor to pull it free. The faster the water and the shorter lead that you use, the greater the chance that either you will error and give the engine too much throttle, pulling the stern under and taking on water, or that on a very tight anchor line a surge in the water's flow will pull the stern under.

Never drop anchor from a moving boat, never anchor from the side or stern. Always anchor from the bow, always pull anchor from the stern and do not tie the rope to a stern cleat.

The deeper and faster the water the longer your anchor line should be. For example in 20 feet of water moving about three miles per hour, about 70 feet of line will be fine. However in 30 feet of water moving at five miles per hour, 150 feet of line might be required. The longer line cushions the pull on the boat and keeps it from fishtailing.

Depending on where you fish and the current, winds and tides it sometimes helps to have one or two water anchors (sea anchors) onboard to use as boat stabilizers when either the wind or current is so strong that it makes the boat fishtail—move back and forth in the water fairly rapidly making it hard to detect a bite on a short line. A sea anchor can easily be pulled in if necessary when a fish is on.

Boating trouble generally does not creep up; it usually happens so fast that only conditioned reflex or pure luck save you, and you can't rely on pure luck! Always be extremely attentive and thinking ahead either when dropping anchor or lifting it. And keep those life jackets on in dangerous, fast water.

The Fun and Utility of Island Camping **8**

There is no end to the enjoyment from island camping, although a lot of thought and planning is necessary prior to setting out on such an excursion. You must plan for what to do in case of an emergency because sooner or later you will probably be faced with one. Be prepared for the worst and expect the best. The more remote the island, the more prepared you should be. There is a lot of fun to be had by all, but it is no fun to be faced with an emergency if you are not prepared.

The first thing to do before setting out on any camping trip is to let someone know where you are going, who is going, and when you plan on returning. The person you tell your plans to should be someone you can trust.

Make a check list of the basic items to take such as a first aid kit and a basic first aid manual, a bee sting kit, bug repellent, flashlights with spare batteries, signaling flares, a lantern with extra fuel, safety matches, lighters, a two way radio, extra rope, twine, extra clothing and bedding, plenty of non-perishable food and an ice chest or two. If you make your own ice in plastic jugs it can be used for drinking or cooking water.

You will need knives, a hatchet or ax, a tarp and a tent or two, and don't forget cooking pots and pans, paper plates and eating implements. Take several heavy-duty trash bags and a roll of heavy plastic film (visquine). It can be a real handy item used as extra shelter or to capture rain water. Of course you will need hand soap, dish soap and toilet paper and a shovel.

Make a dream list of everything you would like to have along on an island camping trip, then eliminate the items not necessary, stick to the basics. Keep in mind that you will be limited to the amount of supplies and passengers that can be transported by boat, depending on the number of trips you are willing to make to and from your launching point. You should never overload your boat.

Consider towing a supply raft, a raft is a handy item to have along should the river drop a couple of feet during the night, leaving your boat high and dry for a couple of days.

Don't forget to take a camera and extra film. Last but not least, use trash bags to collect all of your trash as well as that left by thoughtless campers. Leave the island as clean and natural as you found it.

Skamania Island sits in the Columbia River adjacent to Multnomah Falls. It is a sand island about a mile long and a half mile wide, surrounded by a shallow sand beach, topped with cottonwood and willow trees, having a dense undergrowth of tall grass, blackberry vines and old-growth nettles. A rock-free beach provides a great place to swim and play, with plenty of room to set up camp. Wildlife is abundant, including birds, deer, and if a camper is lucky, he just might get a glimpse of a black bear. There lies off the north side, near the Washington shore, a fairly deep channel which seems to be a pretty good hangout for sturgeon.

File a Float Plan

The float plan is designed to assist in locating you and your boat if something should happen. Leave this plan with the local marina operator, a close friend or relative. (Cancel the float plan upon your return.)

Float Plan

1. Description of boat
   - A. Boat Number and/or name:
   - B. Size:
   - C. Make:
   - D. Capacity:
   - E. No. of engines:
   - F. Color:

2. Number of persons aboard, names, addresses, phone numbers

3. Radio Equipment
   - A. Ship to shore:
   - B. Citizens Band:
   - C. Channel monitored:

4. Trip plan
   - From:
   - Via:
   Estimated time of arrival:
   Departure time:

5. If not at destination by:
   - Notify:

6. If emergency arises:
   - Contact Coast Guard at:
   If not returned/canceled float plan by:
   - Notify: At:

Signed: _____

Date: _____

9

The Fighting Power of a White Sturgeon

Setting your hook into a prehis-toric giant Pacific white will surely get your heart pumping and adrenaline flowing and maybe get your knees to knocking as well. The battle is one of raw energy to see who will give up first, the fish or you. As you fight the fish and your muscles begin to ache you may think the battle will never end and you might even consider breaking the fish off—but wait, just keep up the pressure or let your partner share in the fun. If you are fishing from a boat you have a very big advantage because you can follow the fish downriver.

First, release your boat from your anchor line (be sure that it is attached to an anchor buoy and has a tailing buoy at the end of the rope). Release the rope from its clip, motor slowly in reverse until you reach the end of the rope and toss it in, then go with the fish and stay as close as is practical through the entire battle. Keep your rod in an upright position to allow cushion. Try not to allow slack in your line during the entire fight. Obviously this is not always possible because sometimes the fish will swim rapidly towards the boat and you

Big sturgeon are such an impressive sight. Living to over 100 years of age they are the West Coast's premier resident fish and should be repected with careful handling.

This 14 foot giant spawning female found an unpleasant surprise in her early morning sand shrimp and put up a great fight trying to shake the hook. She was released unharmed. There is no doubt that she is a female; male Pacific white sturgeon seldom exceed seven or eight feet.

will have to furiously wind in line. Do not attempt to pump and crank when the fish is diving for the bottom or is in a powerful run away from you. When the fish is in a hard dive hold your rod up in a vertical position and allow it and your reel's drag to do their job of tiring the fish. When the fish reaches the bottom or stops diving begin pumping the rod up and quickly crank line in as you lower the rod. When the fish makes a powerful run away from you, keep your rod high and let it take line from the reel while wearing itself down against the drag.

Your partner at the wheel (hopefully experienced) should be doing his job trying to keep the boat close to the fish as you work it in.

I say "put the boots to it." Sure, there is the chance that the line will break or the hook come free, but using the strong-arm method considerably shortens the struggle and sometimes encourages the monster to jump once or twice providing you with a lifetime mental image. If you let the fish direct the fight it will simply take hours and hours of luke-warm effort and not do the fish any physical good. Fight the fish with vigor and you can subdue it fairly quickly.

The following fighting times were developed from my personal experiences with oversized sturgeon:

7 or 8 footer: 20 to 25 minutes
10 footer: 25 to 40 minutes
12 footer: 45 to 60 minutes
14 footer: 60 to 90 minutes

A shaker hooked in a fair current or a foul-hooked sturgeon will sometimes feel like an old tire. If you hook into larger size sturgeon (40 inches to 15 feet) you will generally have a great fight on your hands. If you hook into one of those line-ripping, reel-burning, tail-walking prehistoric monster females, you will quickly appreciate the sturgeon's power.

A while back my son Steve and I were fishing up the Columbia at Dodson, downriver towards Multnomah Falls, we had baited with fresh sand shrimp. At 5:30 in the morning I hooked a monster. One hour later, and over one mile downriver (with Steve operating the boat and the camera), we managed to bring the huge creature alongside the boat. Steve removed the hook but before he could get it away from the sturgeon it shook its head and hooked itself again. Then Steve fought it as hard as he could for another 15 minutes, with the drag on all the way. After getting a fair measurement and discovering it was right at 14 feet in length, we released it.

We motored back to our anchor buoy and continued fishing. From then until about 1:30 that afternoon, Steve boated a 65 incher, I boated a 48 incher and caught another monster sized one—only an eight footer! It seemed small after catching the huge one earlier in the day.

Jumping Sturgeon: Large to monster-size sturgeon will often leap completely out of the water when trying to shake a hook. They are often observed jumping for no apparent reason. "Why do they jump?" is a question I have heard many times and one that I have asked, but no one seems to know the answer. One theory is that they jump when in a feeding frenzy. My theory is that they jump to take in air to be used as ballast in order to maintain certain depths in the water.

Bony or true fishes have within their structure an air bladder. Sturgeon have no such organ but they do have the ability to hold air in their stomach or gut.

I believe that sturgeon will sometimes blow their air near the end of a fight to escape a fisherman's hook and line. This is a last ditch effort to make it back to the safety of the river bottom. Often a smaller sturgeon will blow its air after being boated, sometimes in a series of burps, and sometimes with a very loud roar.

When looking for a place to fish as you arrive in the general area don't be in a hurry to drop anchor. Spend a few minutes looking around to see if any sturgeon are breaking the surface. By anchoring near broaching fish you enhance your chances for a faster bite.

Resist the temptation to bring an oversized sturgeon aboard your boat or to drag it onto the beach for photographs and measuring. It should be obvious if it is an oversized fish and thus too large to keep; if you are in doubt pull the fish in the water to measure it next to your boat or at the shoreline (for bank anglers).

Excessive handling of large sturgeon can easily do serious injury. A large sturgeon during the spawning period can easily be traumatized by rough handling and this might prevent her from spawning, resulting in the re-absorbtion of her eggs and a future wait of up to several years

Ron Nanny battles a tidewater sturgeon.

more before trying to spawn again. Female sturgeon do not spawn each year and can skip several years.

Commercial gill nets can be devastating to large sturgeon because of mortal damage to their gills. Unfortunately no one knows how much wasteful net damage is done each year in the Columbia River and Willapa and Gray's Harbor bays by commercial gill nets—yet this wasteful practice is still allowed.

The Fish Tailer

The fish tailer is designed to cinch tightly around the wrist of the fish's tail. This is an easy way to handle fish, however, on larger fish you should not pull them from the water for any length of time because of possible body damage to interior organs. The larger the fish, the more damage might occur. If you are looking for a fish to take home a easy measurement can be taken as the fish is in the water alongside the boat or shore. The tailer is a good replacement for the gaff which has killed or maimed many a good fish.

To use the fish tailer simply open the loop and quickly place the small diameter, plastic-coated, steel cable around the lower third of the fish's body and them smartly pull up narrowing the loop which cinches tightly above the fish's tail. This simple procedure must be done quickly because sometimes the fish will bolt as it feels the wire.

It is not wise to cinch the tailer around the tail of an oversize sturgeon unless you are prepared to lose it. If the huge creature, apparently played out and quietly laying alongside your boat, should suddenly decide to make one more run it will take off like a wounded Brahma bull pulling you and your tailer with it! For this reason do not attach the tailer to any part of your person!

Tailers can be purchased at fishing tackle shops (such as Fishermans Marine Supply in the Portland area) or you can make your own from the top five and a half feet (approximately) of an old sturgeon rod (preferably of solid fiberglass). Remove the guides and thread wraps and attach with epoxy resin a one-eighth inch plastic coated steel cable running from the handle to the tip, leaving approximately 36 inches of free-hanging cable. To the end of the cable attach a sturdy brass or stainless steel ring.

Use No. 18 braided nylon Masons line to wrap the entire pole and cable. Liberally apply clear epoxy resin to the wrapped pole. You can fabricate a trigger release mechanism or simply use the thumb release method to activate it.

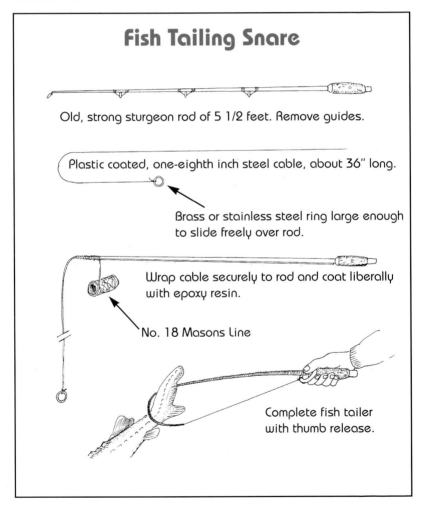

Fish Tailing Snare

Old, strong sturgeon rod of 5 1/2 feet. Remove guides.

Plastic coated, one-eighth inch steel cable, about 36" long.

Brass or stainless steel ring large enough to slide freely over rod.

Wrap cable securely to rod and coat liberally with epoxy resin.

No. 18 Masons Line

Complete fish tailer with thumb release.

When my fami-
ly begins planning
a sturgeon fishing expedition
the conversation usually begins
with: "What are you doing tomor-
row? Let's go rip some lips."
Sometimes the fishing bug is so bad that
I am not aware of any plans until I hear a
knock on my door at about 4 a.m. on Sunday
morning and find one or both of my twin sons
standing there saying, "What's keeping you Pops?
Daylights a burning." I usually have barely enough
time to get dressed, steam up a cup of espresso, grab my
fishing gear and toss it into the boat before we are headed
up the road towards my favorite launch.

Sturgeon Fishing Can be a Family Affair

10

My sons try their hardest to be the first launch of the day
(even if it means we will sit tied to the dock for an hour before it is
light enough to navigate the river). I guess they just want to avoid the
weekend "rush", I find no fault in that except that they consider two or
three boats ahead of us a rush!

Sturgeon fishing for me is a family affair. I can see no better way to
teach a youngster patience; and what better way is there to get a boy or
girl hooked on something other than drugs or alcohol. I have not seen a

"But Grandpa, it's too big to barbecue."

Sturgeon fishermen in the Columbia River near Beacon Rock, Washington.

young adult get as excited as my 15 year old grandson when he hooked into a eight footer followed by a 10 footer one Saturday while fishing in the Columbia River Gorge. Without doubt he is hooked on fishing.

I took another grandson, Shawn, who was 14, out in search of the

great white sturgeon and he landed a very nice fish on his first trip. On his third trip out, he caught his two fish limit, (something that even few seasoned fishermen do with the size limit now in place). He is, no doubt, hooked on fishing.

I fish for sturgeon the entire year and the anticipation and excitement is still there. I am sure it will be as long as I am physically able. Sometimes the fishing is better than the catching but I always enjoy the trip.

I never go without at least one camera. It is great

Starting young? Dad lets little Jenny bring in a shaker.

Grandpa Conner telling his new granddaughter about the finer points of sturgeon fishing. Photo by Shawn.

to come back with photographs of an oversized sturgeon jumping or just a massive head or body shot. Because all big ones must be released so that they can spawn, it is nice to have photographs to demonstrate your fishing stories about the really big one you caught. You just might get the picture of a lifetime, after all, you are fishing for the Western hemisphere's largest fresh water fish and if you live in the greater Portland area they are right in your backyard, even in downtown Portland in the Willamette.

The Willamette River is one of my favorite sturgeon fishing rivers from its juncture with the Columbia upstream to impressive Willamette Falls in Oregon City (about a 20 mile section). Shad and lamprey eels bunch up in great numbers below the falls while either attempting to spawn (in the case of the shad) or jump it (in the case of the lampreys). In addition, millions of steelhead and salmon smolts come down the falls (and some through the turbine "grinders") in the spring, supplying another source of sturgeon food. I have done well in the Milwaukie to Oregon city area hooking sturgeon in the legal size range from 42 to 66 inches long, as well as larger ones.

There is no end to good fishing holes in the Columbia River; however my favorite fishing spots are in the Troutdale to Dodson area. The Columbia is free flowing for 150 miles from Bonneville Dam to its mouth near Astoria. In this stretch of water the river averages almost two miles across. Thus you have nearly 300 square miles to explore! I suggest that you buy a river atlas for the Columbia to help you narrow your search in determining where the holes are.

11

Let's Eat

So you were lucky enough or skillful enough to "bring home the meat." Well, there are countless ways to cook sturgeon, you can batter fry "chips," broil it, steam it with asparagus (creamery buttered), boil cubes in salt water, make chowder, etc., but if the fish is not properly butchered, you will most likely never want to eat sturgeon again. If you decide to butcher the fish, it is most important to remove the spinal cord. If you fillet it you will never touch the cord. The fatty layer and the red layer should be removed, leaving only white meat for the cook. Properly cleaned sturgeon tastes a bit like chicken or pork. Sturgeon are cartilaginous so there is no danger of choking on a bone. The anatomy of a sturgeon is very similar to that of a shark.

The recipes in this chapter are original and would be a welcome addition to the library of any gourmet chef!

From Pam's Kitchen
Skamania Island Sturgeon Chowder

Developed on Skamania Island, in an old cast iron Dutch oven, over the glowing coals of a camp fire. Kitchen tested by "the old man" and a bunch of grandkids and some neighboring campers. Of course the most important ingredient is fresh caught sturgeon, trimmed of all fat and red meat (trimmed meat is most important for any sturgeon recipe). Serves four to six country servings (serving bowl sized).

Sturgeon should never be over cooked, it needs only to be cooked until white throughout. Over cooking tends to toughen the meat. The amount of sturgeon required for this recipe depends of whether you are cooking for two, or a hay crew—too much sturgeon cannot be added!

Ingredients:
1 heavy 8 qt. covered stainless or aluminum kettle
1 or more lbs. cubed, trimmed sturgeon
3 medium white potatoes, peeled
3 celery stocks diced
1 large white onion, diced
4 large carrots, course grated
1 bundle green onions, chopped

FRANK AMATO

2 cans evaporated condensed milk
Juice of one lemon
1 teaspoon salt
1/4 cup white flour
1 teaspoon course ground black pepper (season to taste)
2 cubes (one half pound) creamery butter

Place potatoes, celery and diced onion in kettle, cover vegetables with water, bring to a boil. (Kettle must be covered throughout the

FRANK AMATO

entire process). Reduce to medium heat, allow to cook until potatoes are done but firm, then reduce heat to low/medium low, for an additional 20 to 30 minutes before adding carrots, salt, pepper.

Continue cooking on low/medium low until carrots are done (firm), before adding sturgeon cubes. Occasionally stir chowder throughout process. Add milk, green onion, lemon juice, and butter. Mix flour and water to a smooth paste (the more flour paste, the thicker the chowder), slowly stir in flour paste, stir until chowder thickens. Serve with soda crackers and a large spoon!

"You can't eat just one bowl!"

Gourmet Dining from Bill's Kitchen
Stuffed Sturgeon

To begin, you need one filet from a 42 inch sturgeon, properly cleaned free of fat. Cross cut the filet in one to two inch steaks. Split steak to form a pocket. Now you are ready for the stuffing.

Stuffing

1/2 cup real mayonnaise
1/2 cup grated cheese of your choice
1/2 teaspoon cream of tartar
2 cloves garlic, pressed
1/3 cup grated red onion
1/4 lb. crab meat
1/4 lb. shrimp meat

Combine stuffing ingredients in a serving bowl, season to taste with salt and course ground pepper, gently mix by hand to a uniform mixture.

Generously stuff the sturgeon pockets to form a slight bulging dome, grate another half cup of cheese to sprinkle on top of stuffed pockets. Wrap each pocket with tin foil, leaving open at the top. Bake at 350 degrees or cook on a bar-b-que grill 12 to 14 minutes.

This recipe was created and perfected by my good friend Billy Barton. He likes to couple this recipe along with a baked potato and tossed green salad and serve hot with white wine to make a complete gourmet meal.

Sturgeon Kabobs from Pam's Kitchen

Ingredients:

Cubed potatoes—2 inches sq.
Sturgeon—2 inches sq.
Button mushrooms—whole
Bell peppers—wedges
Onion—wedges
Large olives—whole
Corn on cob—cut 2 inches round
Zucchini or any squash—one inch slices
Butter pats
Lemon juice
Salt & pepper
Garlic powder
Skewers

Arrange veggies and fish on skewers in any order, keeping hard vegetables alternating with fish and smaller vegetables.

Use two skewers per kabob if possible to keep ingredients in place. Lay prepared kabobs on foil. Place pats of butter along top. Squeeze lemon juice over each one, season as desired. Roll up in foil, pinch ends together securely. Be sure to wrap well if cooking in coals!

Place on grill or dig out a clam bed of coals and arrange them to reach a 250 degree temperature. Place a layer of foil over coals. Arrange kabobs on heat. Continue turning until vegetables are tender.

Smoked Sturgeon—Shawn's Choice
Ingredients:
Brine
1 quart water
1 tsp. garlic powder
3 cloves of garlic, sliced
1 cup soy sauce
1 cup brown sugar
1/2 cup non-iodized salt

Desolve ingredients in glass mixing bowl, cross cut sturgeon in 1/2 inch strips, add fish strips to brine and refrigerate 3 to 5 hours. Rinse in cold water and pat dry with a cotton towel. Sprinkle lightly with course ground pepper. Place fish loosely in preheated smoker. Do not pack tightly on racks.
Smoke 4 to 8 hours (8 to 12 hours for sturgeon jerky).

Batter Fried Sturgeon in Canola Oil
Ingredients:
8 cups unbleached flour
2 tsp. salt
1 tsp. black pepper
2 tsp. baking powder
4 large eggs
1 qt. skim milk

Combine dry ingredients in large mixing bowl. Mix eggs and milk with 2 cups of dry batter in separate mixing bowl. (Should be the consistency of a very thin pancake batter.) Cross cut sturgeon fillet in 1/2 inch strips. Dip strips in batter, then in dry mix, repeat this process to produce a thick, crunchy batter.
Cook to a light golden brown in hot canola oil or oil of choice. Do not cook in lard. Serve with a good red or tarter sauce as a dip. Include oven browned tater tots and a tossed green salad for a well rounded meal.

Baked Sturgeon—Mac's Delight
Ingredients:
One filet of a 42 inch to 46 inch sturgeon, thoroughly cleaned of all red meat and fat
1 cup real mayonnaise

1 cup ranch dressing (most important)
1 cup brown sugar
1 large yellow onion, cut into rings
2 large lemons, sliced into discs
2 large limes, sliced into discs
Aluminum foil
2 cubes sweet butter, warmed to room temperature for easy spread-ability
Course ground black pepper
Garlic powder
Table salt

Cut sturgeon in 2 or 3 inch steaks and place each steak in foil leaving ample foil to fold and seal prepared sturgeon. Generously season tops with black pepper, garlic powder and salt. Spread butter generously on tops of seasoned steaks, place onion rings, lemon and lime slices on top, cover with a very heavy topping of mayonnaise and ranch dressing, pack foil wrapped fish in a large covered roaster.

Place roaster in preheated oven and bake at 350 degrees for about 15 minutes or until steaks flake easily with a fork and meat is white. Do no overcook, overcooking sturgeon will make it tough.

This is an old family recipe submitted by my good friend Gordon McFarlane. he won't say how many people this recipe will serve because "after you sink your teeth into one of these delights, you will reach for another serving."

Less than five feet tall, April hooks an 8 foot and then a 10 foot sturgeon back to back and subdues them both with only the help of a fighting belt.

12

The Importance of Catch and Release

Sub-legal sturgeon are caught and released multiple times. Because they grow slowly and do not reach legal size until 10 or more years old and because of a rapidly increasing sport fishery, more and more sub-legals are being hooked. In 1995 Steve King, Oregon sturgeon researcher, estimated that about 400,000 sub-legals were caught and released each year in the lower Columbia system! His total estimate of the sturgeon population over two feet in the lower Columbia is about one million. Thus almost 50% of the entire sturgeon population is caught each year. Because they are slow growing it is absolutely imperative that you carefully remove the hook on each fish you release. If the fish is hooked too deeply then cut the line just above the hook. Use hooks that will rust—not stainless steel hooks.

Hooking, fighting and then releasing an oversized sturgeon is a thrilling experience—especially if you hook into a jumper. These majestic creatures will put up one hell of fight to shake a hook and will often be so exhausted by the time they are pulled up alongside a

To revive and release a big sturgeon can be considerably more difficult than it sounds. A very tired sturgeon quickly becomes a huge handful of dead weight and will tend to become very tail heavy, as illustrated in this photo of Steve Conner attempting to revive an eight footer. After much effort Steve managed to get the job done and the fish swam off on its own. Reviving the fish is most important; remove the hook if at all possible without harming the fish. If the hook is simply too difficult to reach, cut the leader close to the hook.

This spawning giant was caught and released unharmed.

boat that they will roll over belly up. The population of sturgeon over six feet long in the lower Columbia is estimated to be about 5,000 fish. It might not be growing because with heavy sport angling and gill net pressure the number of sturgeon in the five to six foot class is diminishing.

It is very important, and it is your obligation, to revive and release unharmed these spawning giants. There are far too many huge and ancient spawning sturgeon being destroyed through improper handling and through being released unconscious and left to drift off belly up.

Use barbless hooks (its the law) and don't be afraid to remove the hook before releasing the fish. To revive it, roll the fish over belly down, hold on, and move the fish until it swims off under its own power.

Lets keep the population healthy and growing and the sport fishing outstanding!

Good luck, good fishing, and I hope you enjoy all your fishing trips. Maybe we will meet out there one of these days. I'm easy to recognize, I'm the white haired old river rat with the fish on!

Now what the hell do I do?

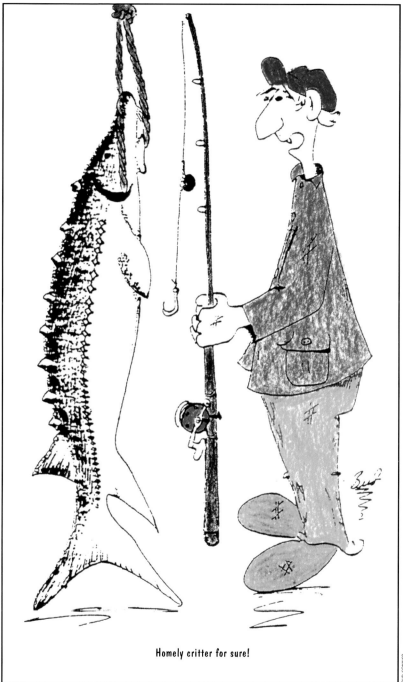

Homely critter for sure!

Boy, aren't they ugly!

There otta be a law!

BUD CONNER